NOW, IT'S TIME
— FOR —
THE NU-BEINGS

NOW, IT'S TIME
FOR
THE NU-BEINGS

JASON BAMBERG

authorHOUSE®

AuthorHouse™
1663 Liberty Drive
Bloomington, IN 47403
www.authorhouse.com
Phone: 1-800-839-8640

Published by AuthorHouse   01/25/2013

ISBN: 978-1-4772-0373-6 (sc)
ISBN: 978-1-4772-0372-9 (hc)
ISBN: 978-1-4772-0374-3 (e)

Library of Congress Control Number: 2012908490

Contents

Author's Note

B efore U become absorbed into what I feel will be a pleasurable reading experience, I'm inspired to explain what becomes obvious upon your immediate glancing at this dissertation. In this book, like all of my literary work, I use the letter "U" when referring to "you". This is not to undermine the regality of language structure or anything of that Nature. I do so because something easily developed in my mind while I was in the midst of crafting this work. A question came forth: "Why use three letters to relate to and describe the single most powerful force in your Universe?" As a tone, a sound, a letter, and most importantly an existing conscious force, I see using the letter "U" in the place of "you" as appropriate. The reasoning that supports this awareness is that in life, in your world the only person that can see existence the way U see it is "U"! No more questioning your abilities (as in "why" which is phonetically the letter "y"), no more doubting surprises (as in "oh" which is phonetically letter "o"), it's time to know that only "U" have the ability to perceive anything and all things the way U do! And yes U do have a choice as to how U will use your perception. U can chose to see situations and circumstances through a positive affirming viewpoint or U can chose to see situations through a not so positive affirming viewpoint. The filter of your mind is only going to yield to U what U chose for it to yield. And it only comes in two modes: mode 1) is what I'm experience "good" as it moves through my awareness or mode 2) Is what I'm experiencing "not good" as it moves through my awareness. I see those two points of reference as the two arms of the letter "U". One side representing what's considered "good" or what "aught" to be done, the other side representing that which is "not good" or what is considered "naught" as in not wanting it to be.

As U can see the journey of a human being whether it be a "good" journey or whether it be a "not so good" journey begins with one simple factor. That factor is "U"! It is my hopes that the motivating energy of positive influences fill your mind, body, and soul with the redolence of life as U read this. It is true; U can do, be, or have anything U create within your mind as your aspiring idea or ideas of pursuit.

That pretty much sums up the purpose as to why I decided to replace "you" with U. I would also like thank U for the consideration U've shown by reading this work. So without further delay, let us begin this journey shall we?

Well, my fellow human beings, there is simply no turning back from this point forward. All life here on this resplendent planet we call Earth is undergoing a very grand period of massive transformations. We can say these are the transformations of immeasurable and unimaginable **Cosmic** proportions. There are many people, in their own beliefs, professions, and preferences who attribute this time to a period of unspeakable magnitude. All genre of ideologies—from the religious to the non-religious, to the metaphysical to the mundane—all have some reference in their awareness as to what it means being here on Earth at this time. The combination of ideas and beliefs as to what is taking place on Earth at this time can seem very kaleidoscopic and confusing for many. Therefore, this **Universe** (God-force, Cosmos, Omni-verse, Multi-verse, Xeno-verse, etc. are all different names for the same thing in essence) finds it necessary to inform each and every human who truly seeks to know. There is a timeless maxim that exemplifies that point clearly. *"Ask and it shall be given, Seek and U will find, Knock and the door will be opened (A.S.K.)"*. This statement surmises the simplicity behind all that is taking place right NOW!

This **Jewel** (literary dissertation) entitled *"Now, It's Time for the **NU** Beings"* is my attempt to quickly provide clarity for anyone truly seeking to peak behind the veil of mystery surrounding this overall transformation. There will be a **NU** heaven and a **NU** Earth and we are living in its blossoming because we are its blossoming!

Q. U use the expression "Nu" instead of "new". What is the difference and why do U use it?

A. NU is a very ancient term. Its pronunciation is "nuu" which is phonetically the same as the word "new". Its use can be found originating from people who inhabited the African continent, particularly central and eastern Africa. The land of the ancient Egyptians was a land that originally belonged to a group of Supreme Beings called **NU**-beings. The Central American continent, as well as many South American regions, were also places where the **NU**-beings dwelt. The ancient term **NU** isn't indigenous to other continents, but there are equivalent terms used by the ancient humans inhabiting those continents that relates to the exact same meaning of what **NU** meant to all the ancient people of the past. To those people, **NU**-beings were a part of the human family whose existence was based on a type of purely positive and divine power of life found within themselves as opposed to power based on external datum. At this point the thoughts of many people drift into the areas of race, tribal allegiance, or nationality. It is a major fallacy to assume that **NU**-beings represent a particular race of people. The human race is one race of people with many variations to its species. That variation is a result of the diversity that **Nature/God** promotes through conditions that go beyond the partiality prejudice period. "**NU**" is a conceptual term. Its meaning hinges upon the idea that pure darkness is the **Source** that holds all potential for creation. It was also described as an infinite "sea" of pure positive potential. The exact location of this precious darkness of **NU** is found within all human beings as the blackness or the black board of their minds. All intellect is governed in the darkness of the mind. Darkness is uniform and eternal. Therefore U are in darkness at all times. Light has its value only in darkness. As a human U are a microcosmic representation of the entire **Universe** or **Godforce**. On a macrocosmic scale the closest notion U can use to understand the meaning of **NU** would be what your present day astrophysicists and astronomers call *Dark Matter, Dark Energy,* or *Space* itself. Because of the light of the Sun and all the many manifestations of life on earth, humans with their physical eyes electively forget that earth's existence, the sun's existence, and all existence is in **Darkness**. If U are a person familiar with biblical teachings, when U open the bible, the very first verse reads, "*In the beginning God created the heaven and* *the earth"*. It then goes on to explain what God created in verse 2. In the third verse something significant is expressed. Genesis 1:3 reads: *"And God said, let there be light"*. This verse literally tells believers of the bible that God existed in a state of **Darkness**, before turning on the light. Those verses in their simplicity echo what was known for thousands of years prior to the existence of biblical work. The essence of those verses and the knowledge relating to the events of creation simply relay a great reality which says; in that state of darkness was the *"power"* and *"intellect"* needed to create such a massive creation like Heaven and Earth or basically creation. All the religions of the world literally relay this same truism. Here are some examples of how darkness can appropriately compare: Darkness is the house, Light is the home. Darkness is the cup, Light is the liquid. Darkness is the blackboard, Light is the chalk. Darkness is the journey, Light is the destination. From these examples I feel U get the essence of the value of darkness as a prime influence of existence itself.

Many people are afraid of darkness. It has in essence gotten a bad rap in modern times. That is because people have succumbed to the fear of life and the scapegoat used as an excuse to explain their fear is the idea of darkness being bad or evil. Darkness is not bad. It just is. Darkness has never in the eternalness of **All** time, **All** matter, and **All** space ever hurt anyone or anything. It is always what is found in the darkness that has been the Source of misery for created conscious beings. And when the "created conscious beings" realize that they are co-creators within themselves, then they will know that what they make happen first in the dark (within) will manifest in the light (the external world). So as a creator, it is U who has the ability to attract that which is wanted or that which is unwanted. Given that statement, darkness is not the problem. It is the fear that humans hold within, that causes the problems that appear as manifested experiences. Know this: U are intimately tied to the **Source** of All creation, and will come to remember this supreme state of connectivity. The process of remembering is what is called "transformation" or "ascension". There is an inner light that exist within the darkness of humans that many call the "Inner Being" or "Soul". When that Inner Being comes to the surface of your affairs, U then become a **NU**-being. U become the creator of your reality because U are the creator of your reality. We will explore this further in our work, but for now back to our original point.

U now have the conceptual or internal meaning of the term **NU**. Let us now visit the corresponding reality that externally exemplifies what **NU** exists as. I should mention that the maxim "As above, so below" alludes to a powerful Universal Law (**Law of Correspondence**) that allows U to see how your "inner" world relates to your external world. We mentioned earlier the terms dark matter and dark energy. *Dark Matter* as well as *Dark Energy* are in basic terms, energies that dominate at least 95% of the Universe as opposed to matter which only occupies roughly 5% of the Universe. In other words *Dark Matter* or *Dark Energy* is the most dominating force in all of existence. It surrounds and encompasses all of existence and gives "value" to the physical portions (5%) of all we know to be creation.

7

Now, if U are applying yourself by thinking with an open mind, U may be asking yourself what does any of this have to do with me or anything happening on this planet right now! This simple point has everything to do with what is happening to U and everything to do with what is happening on this planet right NOW. Let us begin by defining the words *dark* and *energy*.

Dark according to Merriam Webster dictionary means:

1: *a*: devoid or partially devoid of light : not receiving, reflecting, transmitting, or radiating light <a *dark* room> *b* : transmitting only a portion of light <*dark* glasses>

2: *a*: wholly or partially black <*dark* clothing> *b of a color* : of low or very low lightness *c* : being less light in color than other substances of the same kind <*dark* rum>

And the term **Energy** according to Merriam Webster dictionary means:

1: *a*: dynamic quality <narrative *energy*> *b* : the capacity of acting or being active <intellectual *energy*> *c* : a usually positive spiritual force <the *energy* flowing through all people>

2: vigorous exertion of power: EFFORT <investing time and *energy*>

3: a fundamental entity of nature that is transferred between parts of a system in the production of physical change within the system and usually regarded as the capacity for doing work

4: usable power (as heat or electricity); *also*: the resources for producing such power

So when U put the definitions of these two terms Dark and Energy together U come up with a term that simply means that there is an <u>unseen **NATURAL and INTELLIGENT** force that decorates the totality of existence</u>. And, yes, this force also decorates U!

When human astronomers witness Dark Energy externally with their eyes, they are viewing the **Source** that gives rise to why all of these changes are taking place on Earth. This unseen **Natural** force is a force that expresses **Pure Positive Energy** and is facilitating the expansion of All. I will repeat: this unseen intelligent force called *Dark Energy* is constantly sending a purely **Positive** vibration throughout the **Cosmos** that is acting upon all matter in existence including U. The energetic force that I speak of literally has a magnetic charge that is **Positive** making it opposite to the charge that permeates the atmosphere on Earth now. When anyone aligns themselves correctly with the positivity they find within, they immediately become a receiver for this energy as it finds its way into earth's atmosphere. Your presence here is paramount for the survival of the entire **Universe**. U serve as a specifically functioning receiver of this **NU** dark energy. Remember the **Law of Correspondence** states "As above, so below"? What that means is that what takes place in the **Cosmos**, ultimately takes place within the individuated created creatures or simply what happens in Heaven takes place on Earth. So, we can decree a very real and powerful determination that U and I live in two worlds simultaneously. There exists the physical realm (5% of existence) which exists as an extension of the non-physical (95% of existence) realm. The medium in which **Dark Energy** flows outside of Earth is called space. The medium in which **Dark Energy** flows inside of U as a human is called your Mind! The conduit or connecting niche for all of this is the **Inner Being** or **Soul**. This is the corresponding quality of all humans that makes each person an Eternal being of creation.

This knowledge was prevalent on Earth amongst human beings a long time ago. They were and are your family, the **NU** beings of old. They are and U are the **NU** beings of NOW! And they (your Ancient Ancestors) called **Dark Energy** or Mental Energy, **NU**! This **NU** energy that your ancient ancestors utilized and thrived by is the energy of Infinite Possibilities. Please re-read that statement. This **NU** energy makes all things possible! If U can conceive it U can achieve it. And whatever U can conceive is formulated in your Mind first! Ironically the English term "new" is phonetically the same as **NU**. Just like anything "new" that comes into being, that new thing comes from the uncreated (darkness/**NU**) into the created (light) physical world. This **Universe** (Godliness) is now moving in and inspiring everyone to become **NU** beings!

When we divulge into the semantics of **NU**, there is an empowerment towards a profound principle. There is something extremely powerful and **Divine** stirring in (**N**) you (**U**)! It's time for the **NU** beings to come forth!

Q. Why did U place emphasis on the ancestors and what they knew?

A. This is a very important question. Ancestry deals with a powerful and import aspect of your **Divine** function. U see, by **Nature**, U are gifted with a living record of the essence of those that come before U. U now live as a culmination of all of those before U. That living record of power, knowledge, love, and support is written into the fabric of your spirit through your blood. It is called genealogy. Your genes carry not only physical information, but also mental and emotional vibrations of **Universal** knowledge. Genes are packets of DNA material that contain instructions to the function of your entire SELF. As **NU**-beings we benefit from the wishes and desires of those before us. That being the case, as **NU**-beings we lean heavily upon the *right knowledge* that is held sacred within the blood of the physical being. U are born with this knowing. This knowledge is not like an item that U should possess. This knowledge is who U are. The true knowledge of your ancestry extends all the way back to the beginning of the foundation of this Earth and beyond. I will further explain this later in my work. Your ancestors now exist in the realm of **NU** as infinite intelligence, and their return is now coming back into your awareness as the inspiration to be as great and as joyous as U possibly can. The sages and mystics of the past call this time we currently live in, the beginning of "the Golden Era of Humanity".

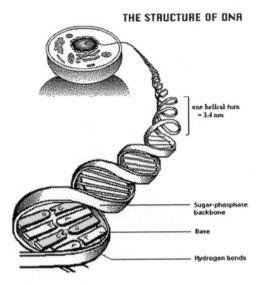

THE STRUCTURE OF DNA

one helical turn
= 3.4 nm

Sugar-phosphate
backbone

Base

Hydrogen bonds

This is an image of DNA. If U will notice, the geometry of the double helix is reminiscent of two serpents wrapped around a medium that allows bonding between the two.

Q. So are U saying that God is Universal and not just a deity found in the bible or religion?

A. Yes that is exactly what I am saying. More specifically what I am saying is that God is the conscious intelligent force that moves through all of creation because it is all of creation.

Q. So is NU a type of God or a type of being?

A. No. **NU** is not a type of God. **NU** is the **Source of All Existence** existing as darkness/stillness. Just as black is said to exist as the combination of "ALL" colors into one materialization, **NU** is a conscious intelligent force that exists as the culmination of "ALL" possibilities therefore it manifests as the dark space of your **MIND WHICH HOUSES THE ENERGY OF ALL OF YOUR THOUGHTS**. U are the God!

Q. Whoa, wait, are U telling me that I am God? No way, why do U say such things?

A. U haven't been studying your religious teachings, nor have U been studying science. They both point to the fact that U are God. Psalm 82:6 states and I quote, " . . . . *ye are gods and all of U are children of The Most High.* Scientifically speaking, there is a new (**NU**) way of dealing with natural knowledge. They call this new science (which is really an ancient science) quantum mechanics or quantum physics. Quantum physics basically deals with the knowledge that all of creation is interwoven and interdependent because all of creation is energy vibrating at different combinations of frequencies. The number of combinations that these vibrations can take on is infinite and limitless. These vibrations are waves of energy thus quantum mechanics is also called wave mechanics. Let's define some terms here before we continue.

Vibrate according to Merriam Webster is defined as:

1: to swing or move to and fro

2: to emit with or as if with a vibratory motion

3: to mark or measure by oscillation <a pendulum *vibrating* seconds>

4: to set in vibration

Frequency according to Merriam Webster is defined as:

1: the fact or condition of occurring frequently

2 *a* : the number of times that a periodic function repeats the same sequence of values during a unit variation of the independent variable *b* : the number, proportion, or

percentage of items in a particular category in a set of DATA

3: the number of repetitions of a periodic process in a unit of time: as *a* : the number of complete alternations per second of an alternating current *b* : the number of complete oscillations per second of energy (as sound or electromagnetic radiation) in the form of waves.

And **Wave** according to Merriam Webster is:

1: *a*: a moving ridge or swell on the surface of a liquid (as of the sea) *b* : open water

2: *a*: a shape or outline having successive curves *b* : a waviness of the hair *c* : an undulating line or streak or a pattern formed by such lines

3: something that swells and dies away: as *a* : a surge of sensation or emotion <a *wave* of anger swept over her> *b* : a movement sweeping large numbers in a common direction <*waves* of protest> *c* : a peak or climax of activity <a *wave* of buying>

7: *a*: a disturbance or variation that transfers energy progressively from point to point in a medium and that may take the form of an elastic deformation or of a variation of pressure, electric or magnetic intensity, electric potential, or temperature *b* : one complete cycle of such a disturbance

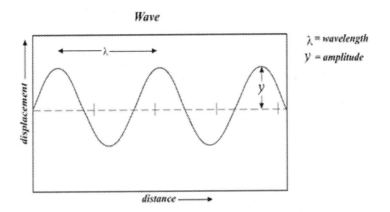

What all of this means is that within the dynamics of your being U are sending off waves of energy that this **Universe** is constantly responding to in like fashion. Your thoughts, emotions, subtle feelings, and your awareness are all vibrations moving at different rates of motion. The

vibrations of your body are slower and denser than the vibrations that comprise your emotions. The vibrations that comprise your emotions are different than the vibrations that comprise your thoughts, and so on. These vibrations are all held together by the uniqueness of your relationship to the *Source of All* or simply *God*.

Remember the maxim we gave earlier . . . ."ask it shall be given, seek ye shall find, knock and the door shall be opened?" Well the asking is a sending modality, and the answering is a receiving modality. Seeking is sending, and finding is receiving. Knocking is sending and opening is receiving. This constitutes your back and forth movement or simply your vibration. Your mental environment is what is sending the vibrations throughout the **Cosmos**, and because of that, the **Cosmos** is responding to U in likeness of the thoughts U emit. All aspects of your *"being-ness"* responds to how U are ultimately thinking. Take the example of a puddle. If U throw a rock in the puddle, the waves ripple from the point at which the rock hits the water. As the ripples expand, they reach out as far as they can, and then a small number of those vibrations begin to return to the exact **Source** or point in which the rock impacted the puddle. So what U put out in thought/feeling, returns to U likewise. As U sow, so shall U reap! Remember this, your Mind connects U to the 95% of the **Universe** that U cannot physically detect. That makes the 95% of your functionality non-physical. The thoughts U think affects the unseen (non-physical) portions of the Universe that U live in. The Universe then responds by bringing into your physical experience the results that U created through your thoughts. If U want a better life, U have to think better thoughts. Remember earlier we spoke about how this **NU** energy is sending a purely **Positive** energy. If U can "overstand" this statement, then U can realize how important it is for U to change as much as U can of what is within U to a more **Positive** frequency, *frequently* so that U can become the **NU** being that this **Universe** is beckoning U to be. It is time to become knowledgeable of your **God-ship** and the only way to do so is to follow the path of **Positivity** that is found within U.

Q. **Well that sounds easy, but times are too hard, it seems like everything has turned upside down. How can U stay Positive at a time like this when everybody is struggling, including me?**

A. Well, that is the reason why this **Jewel** has been written. **NU**-beings are humans who are making the decision to apply whatever **Positive** energies they find within themselves in order to raise themselves, along with the planet, through this transformation to a higher level of existence. U see, this transformation is not an option. We all are transforming. U are pushed to grow out of your human shell of dependency on others as your gods and lords, into a more extremely **Natural** type of being with the power to create for yourselves. Just like a young bird being pushed out of the nest, U too are being pushed out of your old human zones of thinking. This **Cosmic** energy is in full swing and those that respond to this **Naturally Divine** energy of transformation are **NU**-beings or simply co-creators. U are at the beginning stages of a *wave* of **Supreme Goodness** that is skewing in all around U. The chaos U see around U on Earth

21

is basically the effects of an ending to the old matrix or arrangement of human life. The end of one thing is always the beginning of another.

NU-beings live by **NU** laws. These **NU** laws are called **Universal Laws**. **Universal Laws** are Eternal laws. So they aren't really new. They are **Supremely Natural Laws** and they determine the path that **Nature** ensues throughout each moment of existence. These **NU** laws are laws that are written into the fabric or your heart (Psalm 37:31 mentions this). In order to survive and flourish in such an arduous state of affairs, it is important that U fully "overstand" and study **Nature** and your own **Natural** connection to the **Source of All Existence**. No one can do this for U. The **Source of All Existence** flows like a moving river to U and through U. As it flows through U, it creates for U based on what U have growing inside of U. The thoughts U think, the feelings U espouse, basically your mental environment and the emotions that accompany your thoughts, begin to draw cooperating people, things, circumstances, and certain experiences to U.

Nothing in this **Universe** or any **Universe** is in a state of rest. All things move and vibrate; therefore, all things are constantly on a path destined to reside somewhere just to start the journey again. That includes U! Where U are going is called your destination. Your destination as it is calling U becomes your destiny! U have always had the freedom to choose your destiny. And that freedom to choose is what U must become intimate with again, in order to create a greater world for yourself. U have done this before, it is time to do it again.

Q. When U say that I have done this before, are U talking about past lives or reincarnation?

A. Yes and no. From your broader perspective (non-physical **Universal** perspective) U have only ONE LIFE! That one life that U possess is Eternal! Ultimately U cannot be created, nor can U be destroyed, period. Death no longer exists for U as the great enemy but know that death exists simply as a change that can and will happen as a **Natural** translation of your never ending journey. I call that superior state of awareness, **Supreme**

Goodness. This awareness or knowing is on an Eternal expansion onto levels where thought has not gone before. That is why knowledge of life gets bigger for U as U continue to grow and expand from infancy to adulthood. What U gain throughout your life simply adds to what U have already created for yourself prior to having the physically focused vessel U possess now.

When U look at yourselves from a physical stand point, U see a created form of physicality. Your physical existence can be summed up in one word. Your physical body is your **AVATAR**! This avatar that U operate within, is derived from the materials of Earth. Let us define avatar shall we.

Avatar—from the Hindu (East Indian) culture is a word that roughly translates as *"to descend"* or *"to come down"*. The term is in synonymous use with the English word "incarnation". An avatar is simply a physical vessel used by a higher force (the **Universe**) for the purpose of carrying out activities here in the physical realm during a designated amount of time.

Incarnate—from the middle Latin term *"carnal"*, meaning fleshly body or vehicle from which the word *"car"* is derived. Therefore re-in-car-nation is the process of "re" (doing again) "in" (within) "car" (vehicle) "nation" (a massive group or kingdom of people).

When U combine these terms, the result is an answer to your question. Think! U all have had multiple lives. The exact number is too high to even mention. Yet the whole goal of the game of life each and every time around is for U to take the **Eternalness** of existence to the next level. U do so by: **a)** exposing yourself to the physical world, **b)** collecting data about life in that physical world, **c)** deciding what would make YOUR life better in that world, and **d)** applying the full functioning of the **Universal Laws** to your endeavors there by completing your destiny (the original purpose for why U chose to come here prior to birth). This mode of operation ensures that existence continues. Life is a dream! And U are the creator of the dream as well as a participant of it. We are all connected to this **One Superior Force** and I am just as much a part of your dream as U are of mine. In this **Universe** at this time, U are called to become even more responsible for the world that U create for yourself. All others have to do the same. The ones who best attune themselves to their **Source** by applying the **Universal Laws** of all existence are the ones that prosper and flourish at a time such as this (2012 and beyond the beyond). That next level of existence that I speak of is going to be a level of existence that U will have to create, so your future and the future of us all is a lucrative issue. It's up to U and all of us to design it. That's called true freedom!

*Take note: This Universe does not take into consideration whether the thoughts U espouse or the "asking" of a request is for U or against U. This **Universe** and the **Universal Laws** do not operate on a gauge of right and wrong. That is your job as a **NU-being** to decide what is right and just for U. U are the center of your world and everything else revolves around U. The power to create a pleasing world that U can live in is found only within your being as an individual. Each person has this ability as well as responsibility. Thus the first and most important step to attaining a "higher" way of life is to decide upon something significant to U. Whatever U decide, make sure that it is coming from within the desires U have for a better situation. Make sure that your requests* *(thoughts) will improve your life. U get the answer to that by paying attention to how U feel when U think thoughts. If it feels good it is good. If it feels off it is off. Once U do that, the* **Law of Attraction** *will immediately go to work for U in your favor instead of against your favor. The next few steps for U to take are basically set up for U to apply the remaining* **Universal Laws** *and navigate your alignment with your intended destination. This action and the use of these* **Eternal laws** *are going to be the way U operate from this point on, into infinity!*

Q. Ok, I think I know where U are going with this, can U give me a list of the Universal Laws of Nature so that I can know what each law is asking us to do?

A. I will present more material available that thoroughly explains each **Universal Law**. As much as I would love to address each law here, this book is designed for another purpose. This is more of an introduction to prepare U for the Laws of the Universe which will serve as a foundation for the expansion that we all seek.

Q. Could U talk to me about thoughts and how they create?

A. Certainly. Now remember, thought vibration is the vehicle in which each item of existence, as well as all existence, is expressed coming from **NU**. A grain of sand existed as a living thought being animated by the **Source of All** before that same grain of sand exists as a material phenomenon. As a living thought it asked to materialize; therefore, it received its request. It is now resting on the beach amongst the other sand grains that also asked and received. This same phenomenon applies to cats, air, water, worms, bacteria, steel, atoms, electricity, cells, etc. And certainly it applies to humanity. Each one of U asked to be here. Each one of U existed first as thought vibration and freely moved about as thought. Some people say spirit. I will not argue with that terminology, but it is more profound than the assumed definition of spirit. As U viewed Earth U asked to be here for specific reasons and now U are here. This may seem tricky at first, but just a little contemplation into these words will prove to be valuable to U. U came from a non-physical realm. U exist in both the physical and the non-physical realms now, and U will return to this non-physical realm. Again, and again, and again, and again! U have prided yourselves in calling your coming into being, the "breath of life." Well just like the breath U have in your body, the inhale is U and your life returning to your Source. The exhale is U and your life, launching forth from your Source. Inhaling and exhaling is what life does eternally. U just forgot that this is done eternally. It's time to remind yourselves of these facts. As individuals U must remind yourself how special U are to the world that U are creating. Everything else around U, relate to U according to the vibrations U espouse within. Your life starts with U and continues with U!

Remember the age old question by Shakespeare? "To be (exist) or not to be (non-existance)? Well that question contains the essence of vibration. That is your to and fro movement or your back and forth movement. That is your inhale and exhale. For the sake of adventure, U have decided to create these worlds, these stories, and these experiences of being human simply for the purpose of adding unto an eternally expanding state of affairs called **Existence**. U are the **Eternal One**, U are **ALL!**

Q. So do I attract what I think or do I attract what I feel?

U will always attract in energy, the value of what U **feel**. Your thinking serves as a directing force for the creation of what U are feeling. For instance, if U are eager to experience happiness and freedom, U will contemplate situations in which U expect a release of that energy. As U think those thoughts, your Heart (emotional seat) will give U feelings that corresponds to the thoughts U think. It may be a party that U wish to attend, a club, a sporting event, a cookout, time with friends or family, listening to music, a business endeavor, etc. In any case, your expectation of fulfillment sets the tone for the experience of happiness and freedom that U sought after as you decided what U wanted to experience.

Q. But what if something goes wrong? I mean there have been many times that I have intended for something good and joyous to happen for me, but the exact opposite happened for me. What about those instances?

In those situations most, if not all, of the problems U encounter is that U have not thoroughly overstood the **Universal Laws of Nature.** Know this! It is important that U thoroughly overstand what it is that U are asking. That asking is not necessarily done with your lips. That asking is done mainly with your emotional curiosities. U send off the requests for certain experiences by feeling like U want an experience or knowledge of a particular thing/activity. U believe that life would be better in having that experience. That's what makes us all pursue the subjects of interest that our current lives inspire us to focus upon. Life experiences will cause U to fine tune your wanting and asking on these subjects. It is important that U envision all the way through to the positive end of each experience that which U wish to rendezvous with. Create it! Visualize the best beginning and conclusion to your creations. Perform this in your Mind before U launch off into action. This brings into use **Universal Law #4,** the **Law of Purpose/Reason!** This Law basically states that: all things have a purpose/reason for being, and all things must also give purpose/reason for why they are choosing to do what they do as they decide to do it. So this law suggests that U lend purpose to each section of events in your day, and U will become more effective in your creating. This law is calling U to become deliberate more often during your daily affairs by stating intently what U expect to get out of performing the next moment of action that U are going to pursue. So U can say by the simple fact that U are bringing up instances of disappointment from previous experiences into your present experience, puts U a few points short of your anticipated conclusion. History only repeats itself because U are actively remembering it. To remember something is <u>re-to do again,</u> and <u>member-to make part of</u>. So U are literally making unfortunate situations apart of your NOW moment in life by recalling prior unfortunate situations in your Mind as U try to move forward in action. When U recall a negative situation

U bring forth the negative energy of that occurrence. It doesn't matter how far in the past the event happened, the energy will accompany the event. That negative energy is your signal that more negativity is on the way if U continue this route. Now that U know this, if U would through reason and purpose attempt to create a world of your own choosing by bringing in the feeling of your fantasy picture, U would be at a greater position to benefit from your work. When U feel less than the best, that is a sign of resistance which is simply negative energy. When U feel that stream of goodness, then U are in attunement with the **Source** within U. In other words, U must be conscious of your energy throughout your day and night. Always find the positive route to the situations U ponder. Becoming more conscious often will **raise** your **vibrations.** Pay attention to your **Heart** and the emotions that come forth from the seat of your **Inner Being**. This is how U won before and this is how U will be glorious in your successes NOW!

So now, let us look into the *scientific facts* surrounding your Divine human existence so U can know how important your feelings are when U apply them to your lives.

*Take Note: When looking at examples of the **Universal Laws of Nature** and how they work, look into the **facts** that surround and penetrate **Nature**. Facts are no more than what the Earth, this **Universe**, and the many creatures of this realm have created with the use of these **Universal Laws** as they applied those laws to their own lives. In seeking the facts, U will build a firm bridge towards that which manifests **Naturally**, and U will then learn how to become more effective in your own realm of creation. I say that to say this, "do not dismiss the facts (best available information that U are exposed to)". It can save your world!*

I will give U three **Divine** (Naturally God-like) aspects of yourself.

Your Heart
Your Brain
Your Reproductive Organs

We will look into how U are physically arranged and we will look into the way your physical arrangement extends into the non-physical world of **Supreme Goodness**. There is truly a Mind/Body connection that will be honored and respected.

The Human Heart

The human Heart is defined as a contracting muscular organ central to the circulatory system in which the functionality is for pumping blood throughout the human body by way of repeated rhythmic contractions. Your Heart pumps blood, the life force of the human being, throughout the entire human organism. What many people overlook concerning the Heart is that the human Heart is not only a muscle but it is also a brain unto itself. The human heart has its own nervous system. The Heart shows a sign of development in the womb even before the brain starts to form. There are over 40,000 neurons (nerve cells) located in the human Heart. Nerve cells are cells whose function is to "feel" by way of electrical conveyance. The concept is very simple.

Your Heart is the seat of your **Inner Being** also called your **Soul.** The word *"soul"* has always been thought of as meaning Sun, from the Latin term *"solaris"* or *sol, yet* let us look into the etymology of the word *Soul* before we continue. *Soul* is defined as coming from the old English world *"sawol"*. *"Sawol" literally* means *"of or belonging to the sea."* **NU** is also defined as the *"dark waters"* aka, the great **Sea**. According to the ancient ancestors of all Humanity, the Sun, in their time called **Re** (some falsely use the term Ra), was born out of the chaotic waters, at that time, called **NU**.

If U look at the Sun which sits in the center of your solar system, U will notice that it is a mass of hydrogen gas being converted to a mass of helium gas every second. That conversion of hydrogen to helium resembles a rhythmic pulse. The pulse from hydrogen to helium is similar to the pulse or pump of your heart. The Sun is a self-sustaining mass of energy for your solar system, just as your Heart is a self-sustaining mass of energy for your body. And just as your Sun gives off vibrations in the form of **electromagnetic radiation**, your Heart does the same thing through the path of electrical neurons that fire off with each pulse. Yes, the action of your Heart resembles the action of the Sun. Nerve cells serve as cable lines for the transference of energy. They reach out to harness and emit energy in the form of electricity. If U could view your Heart as a beckon of light that emits radiation on a lower scale than your Sun, then U would have a better image as to why your **Heart** is called the seat of your Soul (Sun). U know that there is a **Divine** fire burning within your being if U have ever drank an alcoholic beverage. When the liquid of that alcohol passes your chest, U feel the inflammation of heat in that area. Just like pouring gas on fire!

What I want to express to U is that your physical Heart sends non-physical (electromagnetic waves) signals to a dimension where those signals are being received by a very powerful intelligent force. The dimension that your Heart reaches and is connected to is the dimension of your **Inner Being**. It is the mid-point between the physical U and the **Supreme Goodness** U. Your **Inner Being** is really who U are. It can be viewed as an **Arch**

Angel or a **Goddess/God**. Your **Inner being** is super knowledgeable on all subjects on Earth and throughout all of the boundless Universes. It also contains all the information from your past lives as well as all the information on your lives that U have yet to live. That being the case, your **Inner Being** is able to give U accurate answers to the journey that U NOW have on this Earth. It is the force that is in your corner for good no matter what the case may be. I will repeat, no matter what U think, do, or whatever it may be, your **Inner Being** is there to support your Superior Greatness at all times.

Your **Inner Being** is your guidance in this world. This is the "**Source**" that U must listen to. The reason being is because your **Inner Being** is guiding U every step of the way up to the next dimension of life here on Earth. It is here for U to make sure that U experience what U know to be Heaven on Earth. Remember the saying which became scripture, " . . . . *the kingdom of Heaven is within (**Luke 17:20-21 KJV**)*". It does so by sending U emotions as signals. Let's take a look at emotions shall we.

Your Inner Being and Emotions

Emotions can be described as energy + motion. In all honesty there is only ONE emotion. That emotion is LOVE! U have many different names for it, but LOVE is at the core of all emotions. The closer U are to Love, the better U feel. The further U are away from Love, the worse U feel. Your proximity to Love is determined by how U use your Mind to summon thoughts from the world of **NU** (All). Remember what U think, manifests. Your **Inner Being** is sending U signals at all times for U to know what it is that U are doing to yourself when U think within your mind, witness occurrences, engage in conversations, or even perform actions. Because emotions are described as forces that U **feel,** the only portion of emotions that U can see with your eyes or hear with your ears, are the effects of those emotions as they play out in the physical world. Take a look at a sincere smile, for example. A sincere smile is the result of **Positive** emotions, in that moment, moving that person in a direction aligning with **Love**. Then look at a frown. A frown is the result of negative emotions being expressed through the face of that individual. This shows the world that he/she is, in that moment, moving away from Love. Another very powerful example, is when U engage in conversation. If someone is currently experiencing a distraught state of affairs, they would be inclined to complain about it. U can hear the misalignment with Love in their voice and the words that they use to describe the dissatisfactions with their life at the moment. On the contrary if someone is upbeat and speaking adamantly upon **Positive** situations, U can hear the Love as the words roll off of her/his lips.

Think for a moment. How many times can U recall knowing a person whose life seemed to not get better the more they complained? That is because The **Law** of **Attraction** (**Universal Law #2**) is in full effect and they are getting more and more of the same energy that they put out. Their thoughts, thus their **Inner Being**, is informing them that they are stuck in that shadowy world of dissatisfaction. And that **Inner Being** is saying to the person feeling those negative emotions something specific. By way of emotions, that person's **Inner Being** is saying, "this is not for U!" The intelligent person would immediately do what he/she can to distract themselves from that thought or activity. Just get off of that unpleasing awareness. On the contrary, how many times have U met someone who seems to remain cool in just about any situation. He/she always seem to be upbeat and **Positive**. And in every situation that is encountered, regardless of how it may be viewed by others, he/she seems to come out smelling like roses. They seem extra lucky. The reason being is not so much because of their luck. It is mainly because of the vibrations that are emitting from within. They have listened to the voice of their **Inner Being** often, and now they are reeling in the benefits of being aligned with their own personal and unique guidance.

I would like to emphasize that because emotion is energy in motion, the emotions that U feel, are emotions that are taking U somewhere. Either your emotions are saying that U are on your way to **Love**, or your emotions are saying U are moving away from **Love**. The service emotions provide U with, is just like the signs on a highway which serve a vehicle driver. They tell U where U are going, if U know how to read them. In practicing the **Universal Laws** U will learn how to read them.

Many people who are aware of the **Universal Law of Attraction** will say to U that U should try to watch your thoughts. But that is a near impossible task because in order to watch a thought, U must think the thought. Your watching is tied up in your act of thinking. That is why the guidance from your **Inner Being** is so valuable. U see, your spiritual system allows U to create the thought, tweak the thought, and contour the thought, while the guidance for what U are thinking comes as a feeling in that moment. That feeling is to let U know if what U are creating (thinking) in that moment is good for U or not good for U. Let's use another example.

Say U are thinking of a time when U were at your best. As those images come to your mind, U feel the release of **Positive** emotions (energy travelling strongly from the **Source** with U). If U were to continue along that pattern of thinking, releasing those **Positive** vibrations from within U, your world will respond to U positively more often. U would all of a sudden have what others will witness and call, "being blessed". That is a signal from your **Inner Being** that U are on a path of **Supreme Goodness**! U can walk faithfully in that goodness while everything around U falls into place for U. All is in alignment with your way of being in this world. U will actually begin receiving many of the things U have been desiring in a gentle and steady enfoldment. On the contrary, say that U are in the midst of recalling a stressed situation. Your significant other has hurt U, or U recall witnessing someone being deprived of freedom, or U may remember an embarrassing moment. In the midst of those compromising images, U have closed off your flow of **Supreme Goodness** to yourself and your world. U then feel a void of negative energy which is basically saying to U that U should cease that line of thinking.

There are degrees to which something can be judged as **Positive** or negative. Some things to U are very **Positive**. Other things to U are kind of **Positive**. There will be some thoughts or situations to which U have no emotional responses what so ever. The greater the degree of emotional response U feel, the stronger your attractive power is towards that particular situation. The faster it will manifest. (For more on this subject refer to *"A'HUNU This Is the Key to Life"*, shared with All by *Jason Bamberg*)

*Take Note: Whether U are actively involved in a situation or just simply witnessing a situation, (like watching a movie) your **Inner Being** will have a response to what U are experiencing. The reason why is because the information from your life's experience is sent to your **Soul (Inner Being)** and your **Soul** sees it and determines whether it is in your best interest or not. Once the decision is made from the level of your **Inner World**, energy is manifested in U as an emotion. The better it feels the more appropriate it is for U. The worse it feels, the less appropriate it is for U. Remember this: Experience is the acquisition of right knowledge and right* *knowledge can be viewed as a type of light (electromagnetic energy or thought energy) that travels along your nervous system into your brain where it is lodged in the darkness of your **Mind**. Right knowledge stimulates U and blesses U with an eagerness that literally raises your body temperature. It is a type of light/fire that shines in the darkness and makes its way to the dimension of your **Inner World** (non-physical part of U called **NU**). It matters not whether U are actively experiencing something, or just witnessing it. It all becomes the same once it is sent to your **Inner World** by way of your physical brain. In your **Mind**, your **Inner Being** knows the purpose and power of the **Law of Attraction**. That Law will bring more active thoughts like that which U are experiencing to U. Thoughts become activated for U when emotions are felt in tandem with those thoughts that U think. Giving added thought towards a particular issue equals more energy upon that issue, which equals a materialization of that issue. Whatever becomes activated in your being will be the basis to what is attracted to U from that moment forward unless U change it. The task of your **Arch Angel (Inner Being)** is to keep U and your creation on track at all times regardless of what is taking place. Whether U are daydreaming, asleep* *dreaming, remembering something, or visualizing your future, your creation mechanics are turned on at all times. U began creating before the day U were conceived and U are eternally doing so hence forth. The **Law of Attraction** is in full effect. As U grow in power, U will come to respect these **Universal Laws** with all of your Heart.*

The Human Brain

The Human brain is by far the most complex organ in the human being. The brain is defined as the major organ located in the head which controls all functions of the physical body. It is a very fleshy composite of cells and tissues that harness the powers found in the **Universe**, if used efficiently. There aren't enough words that can be used to describe the magnificent functioning of your brain. Your brain can best be described as a living form of divine technology used by humans and **Supreme Goodness**, for the purpose of processing multi-dimensional information. U use your brain to collect and transmit data (right knowledge) in the form of light (neuron synapse) that U send to and receive from your highest self, called **Supreme Goodness**!

Scientist and researchers are now gaining knowledge displaying the magnificence as to what the brain can really accomplish. Neurology, neurobiology, neurophysiology, and practically any of your biological sciences are broad fields of study that have yielded, in exponential fashion, discoveries which were lost for thousands of years. These discoveries are not new phenomenon. These discoveries are only confirmations of the knowledge that humans exhibited when humans walked the earth as **Goddesses** and **Gods (NU-beings)**.

Your brain at first sight appears as a 3 pound mass of tissue. It is comprised mainly of 78% water, 10 % fat, and 8 % protein. There are roughly 7 sections to your brain. Each section serves as a terminal point for all of the neurons located throughout your entire body. The actual number of neurons (cells that communicate through electrical impulses) are around 100 billion. To picture the size of one neuron, "overstand" that 30,000 neurons can fit on the head of a pin. If U could view the neurons of your body, like Ethernet cords on your computer that connect to an entire computer network, U can then realize that all of the wiring networks of your nervous system have a central point into which all functioning is sent out and returned to. That central point is your brain. Because your brain is the original version to what humans now have as computers, the **Nature** of your brain's functioning is holographic by Divine design. Just like your computer creates holographic images that allow U to see and understand the internet experience, your brain does the same with this physical world U live in. What that means is that your brain is designed to create holograms that give U a sense of dimensions.

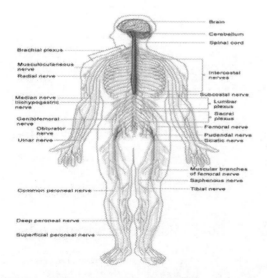

The word "hologram" is defined as a special kind of picture that is produced by a laser in which the picture looks three-dimensional. The human life experience in this so called physical world on Earth has been confirmed to be

The Human Nervous System. Notice how the nerve connections resemble cable lines or cable extensions.

holographic by **Nature**. In ancient times amongst the great Ancestors of All of Humanity, they taught the sacred knowledge of holographic creation. They taught that all existence in the physical world regardless of the location throughout the boundless **Universes** was because of four plus one elements. Those four plus one elements that were born out of **NU** in ancient times were called:

Ta=Earth/Land
Mu=Water
Nefu=Air
Set=Fire

Plus one:

Hu=Divine Force of Creative Will Power (also called Divine Love)

They, the Ancient Ancestors of Humanity (original **Gods/ Goddesses** that walked the Earth) shared knowledge of the Omnipresent **Universal** Elements of creation with their offspring, U. U were blessed with a functioning part of their sacred knowledge concerning the four plus one elements of creation. It was sown into your anatomy and your brain is the central station for this functionality. That functioning part of the four plus one elemental creation faculties that connects us throughout the boundless **Universes** is found in U as your four plus one senses. Your four plus one senses are: hearing, tasting, smelling, seeing, and touching. This is their correspondence to the infinite elements:

Ta (Earth) = hearing

Mu (Water) = tasting

Nefu (Air) = smelling

Set (Fire) = seeing

Plus one:

Hu (Willpower) = touch

Just as all the original elements of **Nature** exist by way of the will or **Supreme Goodness** as **HU**, all the senses of the human exist because of one mechanism called "touch". Light touches the rods and cones of your eyes, U then see. Sound touches the drum in your ears, U then hear. Food touches the nerves of your tongue, U then taste. Air touches the olfactory flanges of your nose and U then smell. All of that touching causes a firing off (light emissions) of neuron synapses in those regions of body. The electrical impulse is then sent by way of your nervous system to the brain. These processes have been concluded, showing us all that information in the form of electrical light is beamed into your brain through your five senses. That informational electricity from your five senses serves as lasers or reference beams which your brain uses to reconstruct your three-dimensional (and now forth dimensional) world. That form of hologram creation using electricity instead of visible light is called **non-optical holography**. Yes, your entire infinite world exists because U think, and it is! The truth of the matter is your entire life on Earth is ALL IN YOUR HEAD! It's all a **hologram**! There really is no "out there".

In this modern time we live in, the terms used for the four elements that the scientific communities ascribe to instead of Earth, Water, Air, and Fire are: gravity, electromagnetism, strong nuclear force, and weak nuclear force. The correspondence (**Universal Law # 5**) between what modern science has learned in relation to the knowledge the **Old Ones** taught their children, runs along the lines of:

Gravity = **Ta** (Earth)

Strong Nuclear Force = **Mu** (Water)

Weak Nuclear Force = **Nefu** (Air)

Electromagnetism = **Set** (Fire)

Quantum = **Hu** (Force of Pure Creativity)

These forces are the basis for quantum mechanics. The knowledge of these forces has been in existence before the human physical form has. These **Natural** elemental forces will forever embellish eternity with infinite combinations of manifestations thereby working with U in adding to the forever-ness of Eternity.

Q. What happens once the electrical light is sent to my brain?

Once the light energy is sent to your brain, it is ultimately funneled to the most central part of your brain called the epithalamium region. Within the epithalamium region of the brain is a very special gland called the **Pineal Gland**. This process of transferring electrical energy and information occurs at the speed of thought. The pineal gland is a pine cone shaped appendage and is the major central portion to your brain. Your entire brain has corresponding hemispheres and the pineal gland sits in the center of those hemispheres. Your pineal gland is the **HU** spot located within your head.

The pineal gland is the master gland of your physical body. Its function has just recently being noted to encompass more than what was previously understood. At one point in time it was only assumed that the

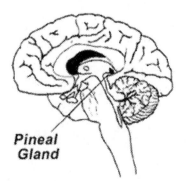

Pineal Gland

pineal gland's function was to regulate the sleep/wake cycle called the **circadian rhythms**. It was known to do so by secreting two essential substances. **Melatonin** and

serotonin. Melatonin is a hormone designed to induce relaxation and sleep. Serotonin is a neurotransmitter designed to operate during the hours of wakefulness and alertness. The pineal gland is known to be stimulated by two forces in **Nature**. The Sun during daylight hours is one, and the darkness during the shadow hours of night is the other. During the daylight hours, serotonin is the predominant substance secreted by the pineal gland. It is a neurotransmitter thus; the neurons of your biological system use that substance as a communication booster. During the shadow period of earth, also called night time, melatonin is the primary chemical released from this gland. This causes relaxation and sleep. There are hoards of information concerning the pineal gland and its activities in the physical world. Yet there is something even more significant that the pineal gland is capable of that medicine has yet to catch up with.

Your pineal gland is what **Supreme Goodness** (The Most High) uses to view what U are doing with your gift of Life. **Supreme Goodness** uses the gland just as U would use a pair of binoculars. It peaks into your world to receive whatever it is that U are asking due to your exposure in such a diversified world of energies. Your asking is done by way of the thoughts that U think. The thoughts U think are stimulated by what your five senses are exposed to. Once U begin to think, the **Supreme Goodness** in U begins the process of responding to your thoughts.

Q. How can such a small gland do all that U say?

What humans are becoming aware of is the fact that the pineal gland is a smaller version of a **star gate**. The scientific terminology created to describe the energy this gland uses is called **piezoelectric energy**. This gland is where human awareness goes within to traverse the boundlessness of the **Universe**. It is also a place where the ancestors of each person's bloodline gaze into the physical world from the many spiritual realms that they exist within. This is what U must know concerning your pineal gland.

The gland itself is shaped like that of a pine cone. The substance of this gland is 90% water. Within the center of the pineal gland is a crystal which baths itself in that pool of water. Surrounding the gland itself is a series of rods and cones just like those found in your two visible eyes. Rods and cones for your two physical eyes are designed to pick up color, light, and movement. Ask yourself why does a gland located in the pitch black darkness of your body need rods and cones? Not only that, the outside of the gland is also comprised of a crystalline structure. Crystals have the ability to translate light energy into the spectrum of visible and invisible light colors. Within the darkness of your head, the pineal gland rest at the center of your brain. Light energy is sent to higher dimensions by way of your pineal gland. The higher dimensions have also been called the **Ancestral** realm or the **Angelic** realm or the **Halls of Amenta** (the subconscious mind or the Akasha records). The Angelic Beings which are the **Ancient Ones** or **Old Ones** of the human race are waiting patiently for human beings to prepare themselves for a greater life within the **Cosmos**. Just like proctors at a university exit exam, they monitor closely the development of each one of U. In most situations, the first angel that U will come into contact with is your **Inner Being**. From there, the rest of the realms of your ancestors will be opened to U. These are just a few examples of many magnificent benefits this marvelous gland will yield to the Human beings as a whole. We will speak on this again later.

The Reproductive Organs

The union between Heaven and Earth, spiritual and physical, scientific and religious, is complimentary to the union between **Masculine** energy and **Feminine** energy. In saying **Masculine** energy and **Feminine** energy, we are speaking about a vibration that characterizes similar elemental components of each being. The female gendering in every species of creature throughout this universe, including plants, has many similar elements that they share. The energy that they share is an energy that is coherently feminine but dispersed through different manifestations. When **Feminine** energy decides to become human, the terms lady, woman, girl, female, etc. are used identifying the vibrations of feminine energy. The terms love, protection, nurturing, passivity, and compassion come to mind when referring to the feminine principles. This energy is found in men and women, but it is predominantly shared among women. **Mother Nature** has shared this extremely powerful force with each and every female human on this planet. Physically speaking the womb and vagina of the female represent the house of the blessings that **Mother Nature** shares with her emissaries representing her on Earth.

When referring to **Masculine** energy the correspondence goes like this: once **Masculine** energy decides to manifest on earth as humankind, U call physical representation of that energy man, lad, boy, male, etc. **Masculine** energy is the **Heavenly Father** manifesting in each one of U male and female beings and is more so described as a directing force. An "architecting" type energy, masculine energy flows through infinite manifestations of all species throughout the Universe. The **Heavenly Father** has shared the best part of himself with each and every male on this earth. Physically speaking the prostate and penis of the male being is the representative staff of power that the **Heavenly Father** has shared with male beings. It serves as a conduit that allows more of your species access into this world.

Take note that when I speak of **Mother Nature** and **Heavenly Father** as two powerfully Divine attributes of ONE **Universal** principle, do not make the mistake that many misaligned humans have made and still make. The **Heavenly Father** and **Mother Nature** vibrations are not separate. They are not at war. They do not look to dominate each other. They are inseparable modalities that excerpt many influential functions on all existing things so that we all can continue to exist. There are many ancient symbols used to describe this inseparable yet uniquely manifested principle. Two of them that I will mention here is the Ankh and the Yin and Yang symbol. The Yin and Yang icon was originally called the *"Shen"* and *"Sham"* principle amongst the **Old Ones** of all Humanity. The Ankh is known as the KEY to Eternal life.

In this day during this age, male and female beings physically manifests as different genders. This male and female split is the result of thousands of years of changes to the human species. The original ancestry of humanity at its peak, was a balanced composite of both male and female genders. If U were to view them, they would appear to be what U call androgynous beings. "Androgynous" is a term from the Greek words *andros*-male and *gynous*-female. They are her-maphrodites and he-maphrodites. A her-maphroditic being is a being with both male and female functioning reproductive organs yet exemplifying mainly feminine physical features. A he-maphroditic being is a being with both male and female functioning reproductive organs yet exemplifying mainly masculine physical features. The androgynous ones were a balanced composite of both genders exemplifying both genders in their physical anatomy. They were the original manifestations of Human ancestry that gave birth to U all reading this material as we speak. If any of what I am telling U seems uncomfortable, I overstand. Regardless though, it is time that U realize that U are birthed from an energy that says anything is possible. U all as humans still have these energies flowing through U. And U must deal with these realities because U are now being re-introduced to the **Universal** order of things. U have to be able to see yourselves in the mirror and realize that U male and female are ONE!!

Q. Are U saying that every man is a woman and every woman is a man?

That is exactly what I'm saying. In order for U or any one of the 8 billion people on this planet to be here, there had to be a union between the all-encompassing energy of a female (**Mother Nature**) and the directing energy of a male (**Heavenly Father**). The masculine principle is **HU**, the feminine principle is **NU**. And because it took genes from both male and female to come together as one desire fulfilling journey, the resulting child has both energies flowing within them. As we approach this planetary shift in the year 2012, these realities will become more workable to U because U will be inspired to overstand your world instead of judge your world. At first glance it may appear that masculine and feminine principles are separate. It may seem that one is apples while the other is oranges. Yet I assure U the only difference between the two is the direction in which the energies move. The best way to overstand this is for U to familiarize yourselves with the terms **centripetal** and **centrifugal**.

Centripetal comes from a combination of the Latin terms *centri* and *petere*. *Centri* stems from the term *centrum* meaning "center" and *petere* means "to seek", "to go to". That describes the direction energy travels as it returns to its Source. U will see the effects of this Cosmic force within the anatomy of female beings. Her reproductive organs are located on the inside of her being because this **Universal** force causing her system to turn within.

Centrifugal comes from the combination of the Latin terms *centri* and *fugere*. *Centri* as we just noted means "center" and *fugere* is defined as "to flee" or "move away from". U will see the effects of this Cosmic force within the anatomy of male beings. His reproductive organs are located on the outside of his being because this **Universal** force is pushing out through him.

The **Universal Law** that entails this knowledge is the **Universal Law of Gender** (Universal Law # 6)! **Feminine Energy** and **Masculine Energy** comprise **ONE ENERGY** moving in different directions. The two are always journeying on a path to regain a desired "union". Once this "union" is achieved, something **NU** springs off (off-spring) and the journey continues eternally. That is a real workable definition of Eternal life!

Listen carefully:

Each one of U whether male or female, embodies the essence of that one being called **The Most High**, or **Supreme Goodness**. Both, male and female genders are hot wired to channel the power of **Supreme Goodness** through their physical systems. As a total being if U are male, the female energy U possess is found within U and your inner world as a type of energy U can **feel** through your emotions. A practical example would be when as a child your mother provided U with food and nourishment through her love for U. U feel that same energy as an adult, when U get those provisions from the **Universe** when U listen to what your mother (**Mother Nature**) is directing U to be **Naturally**. U feel it on the inside as, the positive thing to do. When U do what U know to do according to what comes natural to U, **Mother Nature** (the greater part of yourself) will always provide for U. The more U attune yourself to the

Mother Nature vibrations flowing through U, the more your physical body will begin to respond to those frequencies.

As a total being if U are female, the male energy U possess is found within U as a type of energy U can **feel** through your emotions. The energy of directedness and purpose is the energy of the **Heavenly Father** aspect of **The Most High**. It flows through U as an energy U can use to direct your life in more pleasing ways for U. That which is right to do for U, comes as a direct focusing of energy that says, "This is the path I will take no matter what the influences from others may be." The **Heavenly Father** (the greater part of yourself) in U gives U the strength and willpower to attempt all things that U want and wish for in your life regardless. (For more on this subject refer to*" Having Sex vs Being Sex", authored by **Jason Bamberg***)

Q. It seems that U are trying to relate sex with everyday life and how the Universe works. What is the relationship between sex and the Universe according to what U teach?

These **Universal Laws** are omnipresent, thus pervasive throughout all creation. They teach U not only about the relationships between male and female energies but also the relationship between creating an idea and manifesting that idea. Recall that there is a relationship between asking regardless of the subject and receiving that request from this **Universe**. Well the development of this whole process gives way for the manifestation of the idea and is complimentary to the union between male and female.

This is how it works:

Your asking is sent off into the fabric of the **Universe** by the desires U activate through your thought and emotional processes. Those requests travel *"vibrationally"* rippling as far as necessary (through many dimensions and Universes) while garnering the resources to fulfill that request. At that point, your request is answered. The only step left is for U to allow it to be delivered to U because it is returning back to U. It has to for it is LAW! The time it takes for U to receive your request is similar to the time it takes for a child to develop in the womb. Not saying that it takes nine months. What I am saying is just like a child takes time to develop itself in the womb, your request also has to gestate and grow in the womb of the Universe. It has to be nurtured by your continual mindfulness and focus upon your desire. **Positive energy** (a clear indicator of alignment) towards the focus of your goal is like food from the **Mother** to the child in the womb. Once U are ready to receive the request, it is delivered to U just like a **Mother** delivers a baby.

Remember, desires are your way of initiating your creative aspirations. It is a "longing for something" type emission that is radiating from human beings. U cannot stop your desires from being born within U. Desires are the fire of life. I use the terms "emission" and "radiate" because the word desire is born out of two Latin terms *de* meaning "from" and *sidus* meaning "a heavenly body" as in "star". This alone should inform U of the "Supernatural" **Nature** U possess. All creation is mothered from the energy of desire.

At this point I will introduce to U a higher desire that resides deep within your being. This higher desire can be found in U and the Earth herself and is the desire U have within to be the greatest U can be. This desire is what U used to travel to this world, U use it to travel to any other world U want, and it will be as a fuel for U to continue to travel. This is the fire of life that makes up your identity as a force of Nature. The desire U have to be the **Highest (Supreme Goodness)** in awareness as a human flows up from this Earth into the area of your reproductive system. This energy is a vitally charged **Universal Power** given off by this earth environment. This energy of pure greatness is referred to as *"Wadjetu"* by the ancestors of all Humanity. *Wadjetu* is an ancient term used by the **Old Ones** of Egypt. *Wadjetu* (meaning "green one") is described by your ancestors as a serpent. The reason being is because as energy, it lays dormant like a coiled serpent in the reproductive area of a human until it is called forth. Once it is called forth from the area of what is called the sacrum bone, it flows like that of a serpent through the human central nervous system or spinal column. The *Wadjet* energy travels up through your feet and merges in your root chakra at the base of the spine. From there it is sent consecutively to the following glands along the spinal column where it ignites the Heart. After the Heart is ignited, U then become open to the Universal forces of **Divine Love**, **Healing**, and **Compassion** for all creation.

Once it is received and blossomed within the Heart, the final destination of this Divine life force is at the **Pineal Gland**. Reaching the pineal gland the *Wadjetu* energy opens your Mind, gifting U with reception of all the knowledge the **Universes** have to offer. U at that point will regain your awareness as a **God/Goddess**, in human form. Telepathy, clairvoyance, intuition, psychometric skills, telekinesis, **Divine Love** and other talents begin to make themselves apparent to U. The energy cleans out your physical and non-physical components by removing any blockage within your body thus healing U. From there it returns to the earth by releasing itself out of the top of your head and flowing down your aura back to the Earth. From there, the cycle starts over again up through your feet, into your reproductive area and back to the pineal gland. This movement turns each and every human into a perpetual nuclear (**NU-Clear**) generator.

The NU Beginning

A t this point in our journey I will be offering a few exercises designed to facilitate alignment with how it **feels** to be connected to the Field of Infinite Possibilities (the realm of **NU**). Also tasks will be given for the purpose of activating your Pineal Gland. Once your pineal gland (third eye) is sufficiently activated, U will feel and sense a plethora of creative energies flowing to your consciousness and so much more. This is the energy that will help U find ways to not only survive, but thrive in this **NU** Heaven and **NU** Earth. Keep in mind that these exercises are **Natural** corollaries of practice that will yield results. They are, in actuality, meditations. I've noticed that some people harbor apprehension when dealing with concepts like meditation but I assure U that the benefits of these exercises are well worth the practice. Meditation improves health, awareness, emotional stability, as well as opens avenues for the spiritual and mental aspirants to fulfill her/his thirst for experience. So enjoy the feeling of re-familiarizing yourself with your-SELF. We will begin with background information concerning the Electromagnetic Spectrum. The reason being is because these meditations will direct your focus in such a way that U will feel the effects of **Universal** forces within your being. Electromagnetic energy is mental, physical, and spiritual energy which is the same saying Mind, Body and Soul energy.

Electromagnetic energy and the spectrum we all are influenced by is a Supremely **Natural** phenomenon. Therefore it is purely **Divine** in origin. This is how original thought was designed by U as **Supreme Goodness** or **Nature** period.

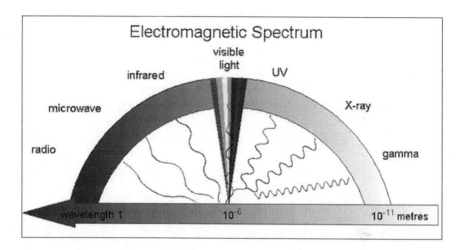

As U can tell from the illustration displaying the electromagnetic spectrum, the ranges of vibrations are broken up into 7 regions or spectrums (some say 9). The visible light spectrum which is the spectrum that is most influential to humanity is just a tiny fraction of the frequencies that decorate this physical world. Keep in mind that these energies are housed and stabilized all around U and within U. In this day and time the **Sun** will aid U in releasing higher EM (electromagnetic) energies from within your minds, souls, spirits, and physical bodies. For those familiar with Christianity, the book of ***Malachi Chapter 4 verse 2*** corroborates this knowledge. This is the scale of your transformation. These energies are as follows (in descending order from the **Highest** to the lowest):

-**Cosmic Rays**: The quantum realm. The realm of **HU** within **NU**, where the force of creative will resides. The quantum realm is a Higher, extremely vibratory substance of pure creation the dimension of **Supreme Goodness** in all its glory, and home to all of consciousness. The greatest parts of your Mind exist here. The frequency range of **Cosmic** energy is off the charts of human instrumentation; therefore, they are not measured to the degree that the lower electromagnetic energies are.

-**Gamma Rays**: These forces find primary practical use in particle physics. They are used in chemotherapy and diagnostic imagery for PET scans. The realm of existence now being studied by quantum physicist and astrophysicist alike providing much interest. Matter and anti-matter become known at this level. Particle and anti-particle pairs are formed at this level. Only higher levels your spiritual consciousness can exist within this plane. Gamma rays are beginning to become noticed cosmically in abundance by researchers. This **Sun** within the solar system is emitting energy of this magnitude in high fashion within this cycle of time. These energies are exciting the atoms on this planet preparing them for higher transformational power.

-X Rays: Penetrate matter, as well as interact with matter. Used for transparent imaging. They pass through matter with little deflection.

-Ultraviolet Light Rays: Very important during this time of planetary shifting. Being very energetic upon the atomic structure, UV light alters the chemical bonds in your body's molecular DNA structure. Mainly your skin is affected, but UV light also penetrates beyond the skin and effect internal organs and systems. UV rays greatly influences your transformation. Some beings on the planet are benefiting greatly from this radiation.

-Visible Light Rays: This range of EM frequencies is what humanity is most dependable on. Within this range of frequency are the 7 plus 2 primary colors.

Violet, Indigo, blue, green, yellow, orange, and red are the primary colors listed in descending fashion. Black and white are the "plus two" primary colors, but neither black or white are truly colors. White is the reflection of all color, and black is the sum total absorption of all color. So in essence they both are more relative to states of being instead of actual colors.

-**Infrared Rays**: This is where many of your wireless communication devices are designed to function. Heat is a prime component easily noted with infrared radiation. Keep in mind that any range of frequency can constitute thermal energy or heat. Certain snake and insect species use infrared receptors as a means to locate food and water.

-**Microwave Energy Rays**: Uses include radars, navigational equipment, and also communication devices. Certain devices create these waves in vacuum chambers for multiple uses. Heating food in a microwave oven is an example.

-**Radio Frequency Rays**: Many describe this as sound energy. Yet, radio waves transmit visual imagery as well. Radio waves show humans the importance of what it means to be an "intune" receiver or antennae for the pure purpose of translating **Cosmic** data. We'll discuss this later in detail.

-**Long Wave Energy Rays**: At this point the energy of consciousness looks to be still, yet this stillness is the same as the High vibratory energy of **NU**. The best example of how this works is when U view a spinning wheel. When that wheel reaches a certain speed, the image of the wheel appears to slow down. If U increase the speed just a little more, the wheel would appear to become still. At that point, if U increase it just a little more, it would appear as if it is traveling backwards. That is what long waves do. They are the image of how vibrations return to the **Cosmic** state of High vibrational energy, just so that the cycle can revolve over and over eternally. These electromagnetic energies are the active movement of the wheel of life, death, and rebirth to more life.

Q. I've learned that the human body has 7 glands also called chakras. These chakras have 7 colors just like those on the electromagnetic spectrum. Can U tell me a little about that?

When we apply the **Law of Correspondence**, U will notice a relationship the human body has with 7 **A'rushaat** or chakras that relate to the 7 colors of the visible light spectrum. The midpoint between the 3 lower and the 3 upper **A'rushaat** is the **Heart A'rush** or **Heart chakra** also called the thymus gland. It's color is green, so when U raise yourself to higher levels, it is the **Heart A'rush** that U are raising yourself up to and beyond.

Just as the visible portion of the electromagnetic spectrum has 7 plus 2 primary colors that it divides itself into, your physical body has 7 plus 2 wheels of light called **A'rushaat** or **chakras** that are housed within your flesh. The word **chakra** is a Sanskrit word that means "wheel". The word **A'rush** is an ancient Egyptian term that means the same. These glands or **A'rush** also correspond to the colors seen in the visible spectrum. They are as follows:

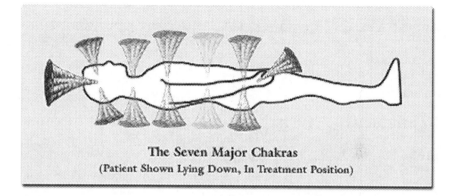

The Seven Major Chakras
(Patient Shown Lying Down, In Treatment Position)

Crown A'rush: The Pineal Gland. Corresponding color is Violet

Brow A'rush: The Pituitary Gland. Corresponding color is Indigo

Throat A'rush: The Thyroid Gland. Corresponding color is blue

Heart A'rush: The Thymus Gland. Corresponding color is green

Soloar Plexus or Stomach **A'rush**: The Adrenal Glands. Corresponding color is yellow

Sacral A'rush: The Pancreas Gland. Corresponding color is orange

Reproductive A'rush: Reproductive Glands of the male and female. Corresponding color is red

These colors are actually seen in and around the areas of the human body. The average person can not detect them because these colors vibrate on higher levels of the electromagnetic spectrum, but U can see the glands that they relate to. When the pineal gland is sufficiently activated, the **A'rushaat** will become more visible or should I say more noticeable. This is what is beginning to take place as we approach the shift. Animals and children readily detect these color patterns within and around people. These **A'rushaat** generate the light of the body's atmosphere called the aura. It is what U feel from a person who stands next to U when U notice their presence before your eyes or ears picked up on them. In relation to the **A'rushaat**, the thoughts U think cause certain glands to become active. The study of these **Divine** colors and how they affect the consciousness of humanity is called *"chromotherapy"* or color therapy.

The NU Meditation

This meditation is best performed twice a day. Once in the morning when the Sun appears to rise and once during the shadow hours when the Sun has appeared to set, are appropriate times. These times during the 24 hour period of the day are when U can feel a **Natural** rhythmic swing of energies upon your life. U **Naturally** "feel" a certain way when U are awake, just like U "feel" a certain way when it's time for U to sleep. This meditation is designed for U to capitalize off of these two **Cosmic** influences that are regulating your personal world. Although anytime when U can find a quiet, peaceful, moment to yourself would suffice. So, let us begin.

1) Make sure that U are clean and comfortable. A good shower, warm bath, and clean clothes are great. Where black or white clothing or both.

2) Find a room that is dimly lit and clean. The room should have a minimal amount of red present preferably none at all. I suggest U find a dark room and light a white candle or two. Candles work well with this type of activity. The gentle flicker of the flame as well as the electromagnetic properties of the candle itself creates the perfect atmosphere.

3) This meditation is best performed while sitting comfortably on the floor with your legs crossed or in a chair. This can also be performed while lying flat on your back comfortably. If U have chosen to sit in a chair, make sure your legs are slightly more than shoulder width apart and your hands are resting comfortably on your knees. Keep your posture straight and **Natural**. If U choose to lie down, make sure your back is straight and that U either not use a pillow or use one that is flattened.

It's important that your spine be straight. The key here is to be "comfortable".

4) When U are ready to begin, take three conditioning breaths. These breaths are basically designed for U to settle yourself. They should be deep comfortable breaths. During these breaths, re-affirm to yourself what it is that U are about to do and connect with a **feeling** of purpose and sincerity. Meditation is not a serious practice, it is a sincere practice. Remember that.

5) After U take your three conditioning breaths, U can begin your meditation. Start by closing your eyes. Take 9 deep breaths. Your breathing should be: a) rhythmic b) deep but very comfortable c) steady. The pace of your breathing should be on the slow side. Slower than U normally would breath. It is the deep breathing that brings on successful mediation. On the inhale, once U reach a comfortable peak, hold the breath. Make sure that U leave the passageway in your throat open while holding your breath by using your lungs to hold the air in. Hold it for at least two seconds.

Your breathing should fill up the lower portion of your abdomen with increasing expansion to the upper regions of your chest. Then exhale. When exhaling, just naturally release the breath.

6) When U get to the end of your exhale, hold that exhalation for at least two seconds using your lungs to hold the exhale instead of your throat.

7) Conduct 3 sets of 9 breaths. Once U get to the end of your 3 set, simply relax and let go of everything. U can even forget about your breathing. Let it all go.

8) Keep your mind as clear as U can. If thoughts arise, do not fight them; just gently guide your mind back to a state of Nothingness. If it becomes hard to do so, focus back on your breathing. Then let go. Remain open to how U are feeling.

9) The entire meditative session should be at least 15 minutes each time, but no more than 30 minutes each time. After U get familiar with it, U can lengthen it to however long U choose.

Things to know:

Meditation is not a rush practice. It should be performed on your time whenever U can do it. It is just like any other form of creation. It works off of the **Law of Least Resistance (Universal Law #4)**. The more U become familiar with letting go, the easier it gets. What meditation does is that it expands your Mind, merging it with the **Cosmos**. That merging with the **Cosmos** is basically putting your awareness back into a **NU** state of Mind. In that stillness, in that Supreme state of darkness lies the energy of Pure Positive Potential. It is your home. It is what U return to. U are that pure awareness

Q. How will I know if my meditation is successful?

There are many different sensations U may experience. If U are new to meditation, the beginning of your meditation may yield little or no results. Stick with it. As your practice continues, U will probably begin to feel better during your day. U may have a little more energy. U will be a little more relaxed about your daily affairs. As U continue your meditations, U will begin to see and feel different sensations. One of the first things U may notice is that when your eyes are closed U will see an inner light glowing within the darkness. This light will seem ambient within the darkness and it may seem reminiscent of moving clouds. That light may take on a color quality. The most predominant color noticed by many is green. The green color U might see is the color of the **Heart A'rush**. The **Heart A'rush** is the heart chakra or vortex that exists inside the area of your Heart. That is the seat of your **Inner Being** or **Soul**. This green light energy is a healing energy. When U are able to fill your being with this **Divine** energy, the cells of your body will begin vibrating on a frequency that promotes optimal health. There really isn't a step by step unfolding of the meditative process. The reason being is because many people are now are different levels of development. U may get results the first day. It may take a while. U may see more besides green light energy. Either way as U continue to perform your meditations U will increase your awareness of the **Inner** world. U will raise yourself,

U will heal yourself, U will align yourself with **HU** U really are.

Q. Why is the healing energy color a green color and why do I see it when I meditate?

Excellent questions! When U look at the electromagnetic spectrum, U will see a portion of it called the visible light spectrum. Coming from the higher frequencies to the lower, U will see that as the visible light spectrum begins, it starts with violet and ends in red. Well green sits in the center of the band of colors that makes up the visible light spectrum. That tells U that it is frequency exist as a midpoint between the lower three colors red, orange, yellow with the upper three colors blue, indigo, and violet. Green is representative of the **Ancestor** realm/ **Angelic** realm or the realm that exists as a midpoint between the higher realms of existence and the lower realms of existence. That is symbolic of your Heart the midpoint of your being where U decide to ascend or descend.

The NU Pineal Gland Stimulation Method

This Pineal Gland stimulation method is extremely simple. But I implore that U not let the simplicity of this exercise undermine the potency of its results. As was mentioned earlier, your pineal gland is considered the "master gland" of your physical body. In times past, it was called the "third eye" or the eye of God. The eye that was held sacred over the great Pyramid of Giza, and the great Pyramid of the Sun in Central America relates to the Pineal Gland in humans. This single eye is the Eye that emerges from **NU** as **Paa Re** (the Sun). This eye is the eye that exists as the Mind's Eye. It is responsible for your inner vision which is the only vision that can encompass your past, present, and future. This is the Eye that has vision over "ALL" of existence. It is located within U making U an ALL seeing being. The abilities that come with an active Pineal Gland will probably require other forms of visualizations and mental application. This stimulation will enhance the influence of your mental world as it relates to your ability to envision different times, places, and dimensions.

This exercise involves the use of water from a shower. This is a great exercise to perform as a precursor to your meditations.

1) Go ahead and wash up completely.
2) When U are done washing, tilt your head back and allow the water from the shower head to land on your skull. The precise location is near the tip or the crown of your head.
3) What U will then do is lift your arms above your head.
4) Next, U will gently rotate your head so that the water from the shower can encompass the top of your head. What U are looking to feel is a gentle

tickling sensation on your head. Your body may even quiver from the gentle tickle of the water landing on your head. When U find the spot that tickles the most, that is an indication that U have located the tender spot where your crown **A'rush** is located.

5) Do not let the water from your shower head land directly on your Pineal Gland opening. What U will do is continue to rotate your head gently so that the water is distributing itself around that ticklish spot where the opening exists.

6) While U are rotating your head, take 9 deep slow breaths. Enjoy the relaxation of such a pleasant experience.

7) Try to feel the vibrations of the water drops stimulate your pineal gland on the inhale. When U exhale, allow the vibrations to take over your body, mind, and spirit. Feel your body vibrate along with the trickling of the water moving down your body to your feet.

This method is very rewarding. This method not only stimulates the vibrations of your brain and Pineal Gland, this method also stimulates the natural vibrations of your entire body. This helps to raise your entire frequency as well.

Things to Know

When your pineal gland is beginning to be stimulated, U may feel a pulse encompassing your entire head. It may feel like an invisible ball rotating within your head. Similar to the soothing sound of rain on a tin roof, the vibrations of the water will soothe your brain, thus soothing your entire body. This is a great method that promotes relaxation for sleep as well as for meditation. The reason why your arms should be raised is so that U can get sufficient oxygen into your lungs. Your brain will thank U for the combination of oxygen as well as the stimulation from the water vibrations. U will feel better. That is a guarantee.

A NU Beginning

In conclusion, we are here, and we are NOW. We are here as willing participants to the development of this **NU** Heaven and **NU** Earth. This planet will be a land filled with great positivity, self-empowerment, knowledge, wisdom, "overstanding", LOVE, peace, and pleasurable joy. We are ready to work with the positive energy that is remodeling all of our Hearts. We are familiar Souls. We are Eternal! **We are NU-Beings!**